How To Behave

Bobby Kurien

Copyright © 2024 Bobby Kurien

All rights reserved.

ISBN: 9798307681923

DEDICATION

This book is dedicated to: My Family

I thank my wife, Betsy John and kids Ethan Bobby and Karen Bobby. They have been encouragers in this journey of discovery called life.

I owe my deep gratitude to my parents, Mr. Kurien George and Mrs. Annamma Kurien for molding me to who I am and my Parents in Law Mr. John M. John and Mrs. Lizy John for the love and guidance I have received from them all.

A big thanks goes to out to my brothers and sisters and my friends who have all taught me something that has helped this work be published today.

Stay blessed all !

CONTENTS

	Introduction	1
	PART I How to Behave with	2
1	God	3
	PART II How to Behave with	8
2	Parents	9
3	Spouse	12
4	Children	16
5	Friends	19
6	The Church	22
7	Work	25
8	School	28
9	Society	31
10	Yourself	34
	Epilogue/Conclusion	37
	Bibliography	38
	About the Author	39

INTRODUCTION

First, congrats on obtaining this book. This is meant to be a quick read so that you can cover the whole book in one sitting.

The Book is titled "How to behave". The word 'behave' has the meaning 'to manage the actions of (oneself) in a particular way' (Merriam-Webster). I have had multiple instances in my life when working with young people on how to interact with others, someone has said these words "nobody taught/told me about it", for things I assumed would be self-evident or obvious. This has got my mind thinking that with each passing generation, this need will become greater.

The next chapter will briefly explain the WHY for this book further. I hope that you will leave better informed and will never have to state the words "nobody told me about it" at least for the matters covered in this book.

Let the book kindle in you a spark to reach out to your world and behave better !

PART I: HOW TO BEHAVE WITH....

As the world changes with each passing day like the sea with its constant tides, the nature of men also seems to be ever changing. The people of today seem unrecognizable to those of a generation ago based on their values and it is observed that those who are yet to come may face an even greater dearth of wise voices and counsel.

A challenge the people of this world will soon face is to find like-minded people who uphold similar values and hence they may face increased alienation and isolation. With the advent of Artificial Intelligence (A.I.) taking over every sphere of life including education, it is only a matter of time, in my opinion, when people will know facts but not how to relate and consequently behave with one another.

It is already happening as you walk out on the street; every human encounter now prompts a plethora of behavioral responses from those who witness the incident. What we see now is that the norm is no longer the norm. Following the pandemic of 2020, we were all informed of a new norm. But a greater pandemic lurks where the fact that there is no norm, is the new norm!

It is concerning but necessary in my opinion for a book of this sort to be written. Parents typically tell their children to behave. But now we must also tell them how to behave. As many teachers teach conflicting theories, many remain confused and most simply uninformed.

This is a gift to you from me. Be sure to pass it on to all who follow.

The author is a believer in Jesus Christ and only offers advice gained from the Bible, which is regarded by the author, as the guide to life for all men in a dim and dark world.

1 WITH GOD

To relate to God, who is unseen, a human being needs a reference point. For how can a human being, finite, with limited knowledge and capacity, come to properly understand an unseen, infinite God? Such a God can only be known by revelation, initiated by God himself!

The Bible is a book, which presents itself as the Word of God. The very existence of such a book offers the opportunity for any person to read and experience what is given as a revelation from One who is infinite, immeasurable and otherwise unknowable. As you read the Bible, the Bible gives relevant information starting from the creation of human beings to the final end of this world. The Bible presents God who is present from the start of creation and we, the readers, begin to travel through the pages of history, through the book of laws, prophets until the Gospels to the book of Revelation.

The Gospels (4 books in the New Testament of the Bible) reveal to us a person, Jesus Christ. He is God in the flesh, who has come to reveal God to all mankind in the form of a human being. Jesus Christ has enabled us to understand God in a way that is otherwise incomparable with any other medium of communication. That Jesus Christ is a historical personality, is adequately recorded by historians. Also significant is the impact that Jesus Christ has had on the world he entered, transforming it from a godless, brutal, wild world into one of order, peace and stability. The impact of Christ on this world, though we have now come to take it for granted, is seen in most modern societies in the world.

In the Gospel of Mathew1, Jesus states 2 laws as the most important of all:

1. Love the Lord your God with all your heart, all your soul, all your mind and all your strength.
2. Love your neighbor as yourself.

The manner on how to relate to God as expressed by Jesus, teaches us that God is a father and that all human beings are His children. The Father longs to draw all His children to Him in order to have an unbroken fellowship with them. This fellowship was broken by the first Man and Woman in history through sin, resulting from disobedience to God's command. The Bible teaches that the problem of Sin was dealt with by God himself, through the person of Jesus Christ, the Son of God when He paid, on the cross, the entire sin of the world. When a person believes this message, that their personal sin was borne and paid by Jesus Christ on the cross, they receive in a divine exchange, the sinless, unblemished righteousness of Christ. This permits them to be restored to the unbroken fellowship with God that once existed before sin came into this world.

The account of Jesus Christ does not culminate at the cross. Because He is God in the flesh, the price paid for our sin on the cross once and for all is deemed complete by God. Three days later, Jesus rose from the grave victorious, conquering both sin and the death. He received all authority in heaven and on earth and ascended into heaven to sit at His Father's right hand, awaiting the time prepared for his glorious return.

Jesus reveals to us a unique revelation of God, that God is a triune God. God the Father, in heaven, God the son, in the person of Jesus Christ and God the Holy Spirit whom Jesus sends to the earth, while Jesus returns to the Father in heaven.

Coming back to how to behave with God, we must relate and behave with Him in the way He prescribes. Going to the first law, we are called to LOVE God with all our heart, soul, mind and strength. If we think about this, it does not leave anything out! We are called to Love God with our whole being! But think about the word used in the command, instead of love, God could have used, a multitude of words to relate to Him. I am sure something comes to your mind now, but then why use love?

The Bible states that God is love. When we relate with God, we must relate with love. We must behave with love. The Love of God is demonstrated thus- God the Father created the world and saw men reject Him and His love and their fellowship was broken. Because of His love for mankind, God made a way for the fellowship with man to be restored by sending His only begotten son, Jesus. Jesus was not sent to only heal, teach and instruct, but He came to also die in the place of all human beings as a sacrifice for sin. Jesus, the Son loved all mankind by obeying the Father and going to the cross. The Holy Spirit was sent in love to instruct and counsel all those who believe in Jesus constantly guiding them in the love of the trinity.

How should we behave in the face of such love? The Bible says that "we love because He loved us first"3. We simply respond to God's love by letting God have our all. This means holding nothing back and letting Him love us fully and loving Him back fully as well. We must also love Him above all things and people. All other loves in our lives must be secondary to Him.

Loving someone involves first knowing and understanding them. It involves doing things that they like and bringing the person we love joy. It even involves sacrifice since it may mean putting them first, above us. Loving God is no different. To know God and to understand Him, we must first come to Jesus, who calls himself the way to the Father. When someone accepts the message of the gospel and accepts Jesus as their Lord and savior, they pass from eternal death to life. When they receive Christ, they come alive in the Spirit and have the Holy Spirit to guide them forever. By the Spirit's help they can have the scriptures revealed to them when they read the Bible. Behaving with God, involves taking the journey with God through love, using all our faculties of heart, mind, body and strength. I will leave the Bible to instruct you on the steps you need to take after you accept Jesus. I only urge you to give your live to Jesus and believe on Him as your Lord. Let him guide you further. He is able.

A word of advice. God is in heaven, and you are on earth. His thoughts are way above your thoughts. He is all knowing, all powerful, ever present. There is nothing He does not know of you. You cannot fake it with God. There is really nothing you can hide from Him. Even your inner thoughts are laid bare before Him. When you approach Him, approach Him with sincerity, truth, gratitude and due reverence, not frivolously. An attitude of humility is best. But remember God loves you and knows you fully already. So, come as you are. When you love God, you will begin to obey God and act in Love!

STORY: Joe's relationship with God was an interesting one. Born into a Christian household, Joe was taught the Bible and the tenets of the Christian faith from a very young age. This led Joe to having an awareness of Biblical truth. However, he struggled to understand a deeper walk with Christ. The yearly events in Sunday school led him to recommitting his life to Christ. However, it was a verbal commitment that did not translate to an active lifestyle of following Christ. As a teenager, he was led the way of the world in doing everything he felt right, though the call of Christ and a conscience that reminded him when he sinned was a constant reminder.

His college years led him to witnessing that a relationship with Christ on a deeper level was possible. Though he pursued it for a brief period, it couldn't keep him away from the pull of the world. College life glistened and gleamed in his eyes, and his life was kept away from the borders of the Church and its influence. In the final year of his college, two untimely deaths of his close friends led him to a pause in his frenetic pace of following the world, leading him to a place of contemplation and reflection. His Christian friend whom he had turned his back to because of their conflicting goals, came to comfort him in his grief. The witness of his friend at this time, led him to a place of clarity in seeing that Christ was the only way, truth and life. His once dormant and sleeping faith woke up and Joe believed and committed himself to Jesus Christ as his savior.

This led Joe in a completely different direction. His childhood faith and his deep desire for meaning was kindled and he found himself devouring the word of God, trying to fill to the full measure of His thirst for God that was parched and scorched out in his soul previously. His life turned around. While some setbacks were encountered, this time the change in his soul and spirit was complete. There was really no turning back now. Joe had moved on from death to life in the spirit.

Joe found out in his life with God that the Bible was true. He received the infilling of the Holy Spirit, and his life began to take on a new direction. Not only was he committed to Christ, but he found himself serving in Church with a new generation, helping them to discover a firm commitment in Christ early.

He has also found this love in his heart for God, ever since he gave his life to Christ. This love has caused him to draw close to God not out of compulsion, duty or any other consideration. Instead, the Love of God that had been shed in Joe's heart causing him to love God differently then ever before. Now his consideration is to please the Father in heaven as he makes his daily choices in life.

Chapter Summary/Key Takeaways

Behaving with God involves
- Loving God first
- Learning about God from the Bible
- Coming to Jesus and accepting Him as the way to the Father.
- Come before him with humility, honesty, gratitude and due reverence.
- Obeying Him as He leads you on in love.

In the next chapter, you will learn…

How to behave with Others, everybody else.

PART II: HOW TO BEHAVE WITH EVERYONE ELSE

From here onward is the 'everyone else' section. Loving God is unique because of who God is. God is sinless, holy, loving and perfect. To love someone who is perfect is easy, but to love someone who isn't, isn't! The second law states it well "Love your neighbor as yourself".

To start off with, we all acknowledge that we are not perfect. We all acknowledge that we love ourselves. All of us who have lived long enough love ourselves in spite of our failures and shortcomings. God calls us to love others like we love ourselves.

Let's begin …………..

2 WITH PARENTS

Parents are the people who a child first encounters in their world. The child learns about the world through their parents or caregivers. The parent's own upbringing influences their parenting style. Due to the dependence of children upon their parents/ caregivers, children have no other recourse but to learn about the world from what they experience and observe from their parents.

On how to behave with our parents, the very fact that we can ponder this very question indicates that we have reached a sufficient age of maturity to consider our response. From an infant to about age 11, while we may slowly come to an understanding of how to behave with parents, it would be mostly natural responses that would be dictated by our environments and personal character makeup.

Parents come in all shapes and sizes. Since parents also come in the Everybody Else category, let's remind ourselves that perfect parents do not exist. However, it is important to note that God calls himself our Father. This intersection of God and his relationship with man, taking on this title 'Father' causes a stir in the understanding in this matter. The word 'family' is also defined in the relationship with God and his people.

Perhaps it's always best to start at the beginning of things! Let's look at God as a parent. God as a father had created man and placed him in an environment of safety and provision. He was given some commands to obey and some tasks to do, implying responsibility. Man had a good communion with his Father God, through communication about all matters in his world. Given the fact that the first man was already brought into a created world, it would require a certain dependence on God the Father for direction, advice and even protection. This would have generated respect, trust and obedience to God, as man explored this vast new world. The Bible also indicates a secure sense of identity and acceptance by God as noted in man's naming of the animals and God's acceptance of such names. Considering this was the first parent relationship that ever existed, how should a person behave with their parents?

Firstly, with respect and honor. No matter how the parent may seem in your eyes, we must behave toward our parents with respect and honor. Now, as I stated earlier, it may seem in many instances, especially with children who are abandoned etc., that parents are deemed not worthy of respect. However good or bad one's parents may be perceived to be, it is well to remember that we live in a broken world. Perfection has not been attained and hence mistakes will be ever present. Even in well-functioning families, each child is different, with different needs and perspectives and the very same parent may be perceived differently by the different children.

As children our greatest duty is to respect and honor our parents, since without this we cannot progress in life. Just like how our parents are the doorway for this life, they are also the doorway for our blessing and progress in this life. Since parents / caretakers are necessary for any human being to grow and live, no adult can claim to say that they have grown without the care of some caregivers. Not respecting or honoring our parents is an act of ingratitude that is self-defeating to our progress in life. So, it is essential to let go of all feelings of hate and bitterness so that healing can begin in our heart. God puts a nurturing heart within a parent and even if parents choose to ignore or disregard, it is a truth that no person can reach a place of adulthood without someone (either their own parent or a caretaker, teacher etc.) being a parent to them in their infancy.

By choosing to not honor our parents, however unworthy of honor they may seem in our eyes, it still reeks of ungratefulness to those who have parented us over the years. We must also recognize that parenting is a great responsibility delegated to parents by God. While parents who fail to value and fulfill that call will have to answer to God themselves, we, as children, by honoring our parents, indirectly honor God who is the father of all mankind. Also finding peace with one's parents assists us to find peace with God our Father and to come to know, love and obey him. A father or mother's blessing is key to succeeding in life. So, seek it out and you will find healing.

STORY: Joe had great parents. They got him whatever he wanted. He just needed to whine and stomp his feet, and he pretty much had every toy he really 'wanted'. They loved him and never troubled him at all. Since they were great people, he never had an issue with either people or resources around him. But perhaps, he took the gifts for granted and them too. Joe did not appreciate the struggles they encountered or the pains they took to raise him. He carried on in his selfish lifestyle constantly requiring things which they would provide.

When he went to college, he found a life different to the home atmosphere. He was so used to getting everything handed to him, he didn't know how to live independently. He kept his communication with his parents cordial. However, he too was slowly realizing that he needed to get closer and better understand his parents.

After college, he tried several jobs and eventually landed a job close to where he lived. So, he moved back home. Since coming to Christ, joe realized that his relationship with his parents have to be God honoring. He found his parents very open and supportive of his ventures. Even when he got married, his parents loved and supported his family. Joe slowly realized that his parents were there all along loving him through his various phases and the delay was only self-inflicted. Joe learned to love them from their unconditional love that he felt throughout his various stages of development.

Chapter Summary/Key Takeaways

Behave with your parents:

- With honor and respect
- Considering them as delegated by God, your heavenly father, to parent you. .
- With forgiveness, trust and love.
- By seeking their blessing on your life

In the next chapter, you will learn…

How to behave with your spouse

3 WITH YOUR SPOUSE

Your spouse is that 'one person' unlike anyone else on this earth. The Bible states that He/She is the person who is 'one' with you. So, for a married couple, they are not two but one.

In this world it is generally very difficult to see/notice anyone but yourself. Your dreams, desires, fears are mostly all that occupies one's mind. To be able to look past ourselves and consider someone else as significant is something most people will never properly understand and adopt in their entire lifetime.

When we walk back to the beginning of such marital relationships, we see the first man in the garden who had fellowship with God and dominion over creation. However, it is noted that no comparable companion was found for him in creation and in that sense, he was alone. So, God puts the man into a deep sleep, takes one of his ribs and fashions out of it a woman, who is then presented to the man. The man instantly recognizes the woman as a part of him and takes her to be his wife and they are recognized as being one. This is the first marital relationship in the world as recorded in the Bible. Further in the garden it is noted that sin entered the world through disobedience and the woman first eats of a forbidden fruit and gives it to the man who also eats. In this way both recognize that they are different, because of this disobedience. The consequences of this brings some curses from God. God also subjects the woman to the rule of her husband.

When Christ comes, He begins stating that He is the bridegroom[1], and we later understand that the Church is his bride. The Bible further teaches that husbands are to love their wives as Christ loved the Church, giving himself up for her, His bride.[2] The Bible also teaches wives to submit to their husbands, as to the Lord.[3] Such concepts elevate the marriage relationship to a divine portrayal of the relationship between Christ and the Church. This is why divorce is hated by God, since He is faithful and does not abandon His spouse. God also calls His spouse to be faithful and holy unto Him.

It is in this setting that every married couple enters into their relationship. Even if the reader is of a different faith, the assumptions and expectations of marriage when a man and woman marry reflects at least partly if not fully, the love and interaction found in the Bible. The author advocates that behaving toward your spouse as commanded in the Bible, brings the most joy and fulfillment to the marriage relationship. It is also important to state that the Bible only advocates a marriage relationship between a man and a woman. Accordingly, no other arrangement for marriage is permitted except between a man and a woman.

In that order, a man is called to love like Christ. Let us look at how Christ loved the Church.

- He led by way of example.
- He sacrificed himself on the cross to save His bride, the Church and to purify her.
- He hears the prayers of the Church.
- He prays for the Church.
- He loves enough to confront and correct his bride for matters involving purity.
- He is patient with the Church.
- He is vulnerable and approachable.
- He is fiercely protective and will not allow anything to harm His church.
- He is faithful to her.
- He does not abandon or forsake her.
- He keeps His promises to her.

These are the ways that Christ loves His bride, the Church. These are ways that a man must love His wife as well. It may seem challenging and nearly impossible. But with God' help it can be accomplished, but God's help is vital for success.

For a wife, how should she behave with her husband? The Bible states that wives are to submit to their own husbands as they do to the Lord Jesus.3 Wives are also called to respect their husbands.4 It may be good to focus on those 2 words, submit and respect. Submit may also mean 'be subject to'. Today with the independence people enjoy in society, to submit or be subject to someone may be challenging to fulfill. But it is important to note that the woman was created as a helpmate suitable and complementary for man. In this relationship, there are certain roles, that when fulfilled lead to harmony and a witness of the divine design, to the world. It is not that a woman is to be less or reduce herself or her personality or her self-respect, but instead along with all the beauty and essence of a woman, a wife relates to her husband submitting and respecting him. In this submitting, the woman does not reduce herself but elevates herself to be the prize of the relationship. When she submits out of love, out of divine power, out of obedience to Christ, she steps into this new world of marriage, as a fragrant display of God's love that reflects God's nature. Jesus being God came down to serve His beloved. His beloved responds to His love by submitting to Him, recognizing His selfless love for her. She lives in admiration and respect for the one who would willingly lay down His life for her.

When both partners do their part in this relationship, it looks like heaven on earth. Both partners will only be able to fulfill their roles with the continual presence and help that they receive from God.

STORY: After finding a good job and reasonably settling down, Joe was in search of a wife. He did not have to wait long. A mutual friend mentioned a girl and Joe went and met her. For Joe the decision was instant. He wanted to get married to this girl! They eventually did. Joe being a believer thought that he was a good guy. This was until he got married! Soon he found himself second guessing his own decisions. Many decisions he took in the early stage of the marriage soon revealed to himself the selfish nature of his own heart. His wife was a woman of good character and waited for God to convince Joe instead of trying on her own. Joe soon surrounded by the love and acceptance he received both from God and his spouse began to change.

His decisions started changing to accommodate his wife's interests too. Making decisions that were mutually acceptable instead of his own. Children came into their lives, but their marriage relationship only grew stronger. The fact that Joe's wife already knew the Lord and that their marriage foundation was built on Christ made a significant impact. Joe and his wife made it a practice early on to pray together at the start and end of the day. All these helped the marriage in growing. While joe knows that he is not fully there yet, he is aware of that fact that he is on the right path.

Chapter Summary/Key Takeaways

When behaving with spouses

- A husband is to love his wife as Christ loved the Church and gave himself up for her.
- A wife is to submit and respect her husband.
- When both fulfill their roles, we will see heaven on earth is every home and family.

In the next chapter, you will learn...

How to behave with children..

4 WITH YOUR CHILDREN

Children are a clean slate given to their parents to inscribe the direction for their lives. Humans uniquely have the power to shape the lives of their young and guide them toward a goal or life direction. Small children are like sponges absorbing everything demonstrated to them by their parents / caregiver. The Bible says, "Train up a child in the way they should go and when they are old, they will not depart from it."

Parents have a multifaceted role as a provider, trainer, coach, life coach etc. to help the children achieve their dreams. This will require a significant investment of effort and time to help their children develop into loving and mature people. Both parents (Father & Mother) must spend time with their children doing things the children love as they grow up.

Young children love to be spoken to by their parents. They love music, playing games, dancing and such activities. Activities which are fun for the child are excellent learning portals. Teaching them through fun activities helps both the adults and children bond and these lessons will not be easily forgotten.

As children grow older, they begin to form opinions about tasks and everyday matters. They will naturally gravitate towards things and activities that interest them. They will typically act as the adults in their life have modelled them. It is observed that many parents wait too long to train or counsel their children, but the early formative years are best to help communicate to the children on important values and for general skill development. With age, the interests and attitudes of the children will change and often only what is already established early on remains.

Learning is a gift that every parent can give a child. A child like a sponge will learn pretty much anything the adult can teach them. A parent should understand that they have the role of a teacher and that in their hands, they have the keys to learning. If learning is despised by the parent or not properly attended to, the child too will pick up such attitudes and lose interest in learning. Learning is also a discipline which if introduced early in a fun manner does not become difficult for the child to imbibe and adhere to as time goes by. A simple habit of reading with the children can kickstart a lifelong love of reading and simply put, everything about education rests on reading to understand. Once a child is interested, loves to read and has a positive experience with reading, they will be ready to go into any formal program of education and like the experience. A child who has less interaction with books and other reading material will have to play catch up from 'day one' of their interaction with their peers. A sense of frustration, when others catch on quicker, can demotivate the child to slowly start losing interest in the entire educational process, causing stress through the whole school period.

Parents should take care not to burden their children with their own unfulfilled expectations. Instead, they should 'grow up' with their child and explore the world through their eyes, keenly observing the child for their natural inclinations and personalities as well as guiding them as necessary. Forcing upon a child one's own expectations and norms without helping the child understand its value or reasoning, simply frustrates the experience for both the child and adult.

Gift your child a happy childhood. It is in your power. The whole world will be blessed by it.

As children grow to tweens and teens, the parents should have established both trust and a safe space with them by then. If the habit of interacting with the child through play and other regular learning activities has become a norm, parents can further begin to share real world issues that the children and even adults may be facing. Talking with your children about issues that they will face in the outside world prepares them for adulthood and maturity. This is preferable instead of shoving sensitive matters 'under the carpet' so to speak and leaving the education of your child to society, which often gives mixed signals, about most such matters.

The act of parenting does not stop. Ever. As the children grow even to adulthood, their attitudes toward their parents change. Even then a parent has a unique voice which if used appropriately can be a reassuring and calming voice to their child, offering them courage and faith to take on challenges. As can be read from the chapter on parents, The blessing of a parent matters significantly to a child and parents need to make sure they speak words of blessing and faith and not of cursing and fears over their children.

STORY: God blessed Joe with 2 children. A boy and a girl. Having children truly put Joe on the pathway of realizing how much of life is out of man's control. Also, the grace needed to raise these children put both Joe and his wife, Maria, on their knees often in prayer. The joy of raising an infant and seeing them grow is an amazing experience. Joe made sure that both his children knew the Lord from a young age. He would explore any avenue to help them grow in wisdom, stature and favor with both God and man.

The children grew up fast. They became like him and his wife soon. Joe enjoyed their company and the fruit of their knowing the lord blessed Joe's home constantly.

Chapter Summary/Key Takeaways

When behaving with children
- Start engaging with them early on.
- Make every encounter fun and interesting.
- Never stop teaching and mentoring your children
- Model right behavior yourself.
- Speak words of blessing over your children

In the next chapter, you will learn…

How to behave with Friends .

5 WITH YOUR FRIENDS

Friends add to life, what salt or spices add to a dish, flavor! Friends are people who make our lives different, interesting and add sparkle. Without friends one can still live and function but having them makes our lives much more meaningful.

Our earliest exposure to friendships is with our parents itself. When parents play with their children, they ignite a feeling that carries over into our relationship with peers to deal with them in a friendly manner. Children may typically find their earliest friends after parents, in their siblings. It is often with siblings that children encounter peers and how to relate to them.

Following that, it is at school that we make our first friends who aren't family. We typically associate and interact with those who we see as compatible to ourselves. It is an organic process. We make several acquaintances but with some among them we become closer due to our compatibility. Similar values, goals, natures attract friends to us. Some we end up keeping as friends for life.

With friends one must be both careful and intentional. Like iron sharpens iron, friends have the ability to make us better people. However, they can also bring us down. So, it is necessary to be reasonably cautious and intentional as we maintain and proceed in deepening friendships with others.

Too often people simply befriend and keep people close on account of their past history or current circumstances like being roommates etc. without first evaluating common and shared values that the other person possesses. This leads one to going places where they may not want to go and will lead to difficulties and strained relationships down the road. It is better to be aware that all people cannot be a good friend to you, and that such a choice should be an intentional one based on your values and goals.

Having stated that, once we call someone our friend, we must be prepared for both the good and bad that we may encounter. In our broken world, we will see and even sometimes exhibit both our good and bad sides with our friends. So, we must learn to be honest, loving and forgiving with our friends. Patience and honesty help both us and our friends better ourselves.

The journey may seem stiff and awkward in the beginning. However, as we give ourselves in friendship and deal with mutual respect and build trust, we gain something of far more value than what we had possessed individually. Also, life without friends does look lonely. So, these initial jitters and slight irritations need to be overlooked as we take steps to build friendships. Gestures of friendship which include activities that share common interests, meals etc. build a base for interactions to occur and friendships to develop.

If we find after an extended period of time that the interactions do not progress toward aligned values and mutual benefit but instead toward strain and friction, then it may be advisable to evaluate the same mutually. Friendships must generally contribute to a sense of joy and peace and when such feelings are replaced with anger and stress on a prolonged basis, a serious rethinking is necessary.

It is also noteworthy that one's spouse must also be their friend. The marriage relationship is also one of friendship and provides ground for a deep friendship if both partners work towards it. Without being able to call their spouse their friend, one cannot properly enjoy the good gift of life, so that must also be a consideration when choosing a spouse.

Care must be taken when maintaining friendships with people of the opposite gender. Especially for married persons, the closeness that may be shared with people of the opposite gender other than your spouse, may need certain boundaries that are clear and well defined. Even with friends of the same gender, certain sensitive topics like dealing with one's spouse etc. need careful consideration prior to sharing such details with friends.

STORY: Joe had good friends. But he wasn't one himself. He kind of looked out only for himself. He had a lot of acquaintances and was a very amiable person. The friendly sort. When he came to the Lord, he realized what it meant to be a friend. He thought a friend was one who never said no to you. He thought a friend means going ahead with anything one says. He realized that a friend was someone who looked out for you in the best way. Who thought no evil of you. Who forgave you and gave you a second chance.

It was truly interesting for Joe to realize the meaning of friendships from family. He learned from his wife that a friend does not have to say yes and agree to your every request. He learned that it's ok to disagree and it's ok to have a quarrel if you care about your friend. He learned from his children that the best fun times are when you simply spend time in each other's presence, that everything does not have to be planned and have an agenda. He learned from his parents that friendships can cross age barriers. He learned from his God that all friendships and even their shortcomings point us to the one friend who gave up his life for him. He learnt that even God looks out for friends and that we are all called to be one. He learned from his friends that sometimes it's more important to be a friend than to seek better companions.

The demand of friendship is not one a person can fulfill without divine help. No one can be a true friend Joe realized unless he has a divine touch of God on his heart. That selfish streak must first be broken without which one cannot see past one's own pressing needs. When the selfless love of God comes in sight, it both inspired and reminded Joe of the high calling of friendship.

Chapter Summary/Key Takeaways

When behaving with friends
- Family are our earliest friends.
- Making friends must be intentional based on your shared values and goals.
- Our friendships contain both good and bad experiences.
- Gestures of friendship which include activities that share common interests, meals etc. build a base for interactions to occur and friendships to develop.
- Prolonged periods of strain and friction in the relationship may need a reevaluation on a mutual basis.
- One must be able to call one's spouse their friend.
- Friendship with those of the opposite gender, especially for married persons, must have clear and well-defined limits.

In the next chapter, you will learn…

How to behave with the Church .

6 AT CHURCH

The Church, for a Christian, is a place where they go to worship God, listen to the Word of God, fellowship with other believers and serve others in ministry. While the above statement refers to the physical location where believers gather to worship God, the term Church also refers to the body of universal believers of whom Christ is the head. In the latter description, the individual believer is a member of this body and is part of the family of God.

God uses the Church to reach out to the world to be his hands and feet and share His message of love and reconciliation through Christ, to all people. The Church also acts like a hospital where the wounded and broken hearted come and receive their healing through an encounter with Jesus Christ as their savior, through the ministry of the Church.

All believers in a church are part of the body of Christ and relate to one another as brothers and sisters in the family of God. The one Holy Spirit who moves within all believers directs and aligns our hearts to unity and fellowship as we come to God, through Jesus Christ. At Church, all believers are counted as part of the body and so no one part of the body can claim that they are more important than another. Just like the body, the various parts are different yet are part of and so consequently, one body. This freedom and care when dealing with one another must be evident and present in any church.

The Church was birthed by the ministry of the Lord Jesus Christ. It is made up of the body of believers who follow the Great Commission of making disciples of all nations, baptizing them in the name of the Father and of the Son Jesus and of the Holy Spirit, teaching them to obey all the teachings of Jesus. This act of the Church of making disciples is a continual ministry of the Church. Hence it is important for every believer to continue to attend Church both for the fellowship and for their spiritual growth.

It is important for every believer to prioritize God above everything else in their lives. Following God and the responsibility toward one's family comes before the ministry of the Church and the activities associated with it. Everyone should be careful not to neglect devotion to God and care of one's family in the service and time allocated to serving at Church.

STORY: Joe never understood the reason to go to church. Coming from a liturgical church, the liturgy literally was another language to him. He barely understood the rituals but growing up in the Church, he came to a general awareness of what it was about though without any emotional or personal connection to the same. His relationship with God also consequently reflected the same sense of pattern. A distant and general awareness without much closeness.

His college life led him to attend a Christian fellowship that was led by college students. Something was different here. Joe found himself crying during the worship with an increased awareness of God. He felt the difference from what he was used to previously. However, Joe did not attend long enough to let it affect him. Years later when he committed his life to Jesus, he started enjoying the fellowship services.

His vocation took him back to his home and attending His home church. But by now, he knew God and that made a world of difference. The mode or pattern of service did not make much difference to him now. Just like the house of your friend does not make much difference to you, since it's the depth of your friendship that matters. Whether your friend's house is a palatial one or modest, it feels like your home too, welcome!

Joe understood also that fact that the church is not about the building, nor its mode of worship or service. But along with God it's also about the people of God. Loving them is loving the Church.

Chapter Summary/Key Takeaways

When behaving at Church:

- While Church refers to the physical location where believers gather to worship God, the term Church also refers to the body of universal believers of whom Christ is the head.
- All believers in a church are part of the body of Christ and relate to one another as brothers and sisters in the family of God.
- This act of the Church of making disciples is a continual ministry of the Church.
  - It is important for every believer to continue to attend Church both for the fellowship and for their spiritual growth.

In the next chapter, you will learn…

How to behave with at Work.

7 AT WORK

Work is a privilege and a responsibility. In the first book of the Bible, Genesis, God had already allocated work to Adam, the first man, in the garden of Eden. But after the fall of man by sin, God cursed the ground so that much more labor and effort would be needed to be put in to bear fruit.

Today, many people find life's purpose and identity in their work. However, work need not define one's identity and character. On the contrary, one's character must be reflected in one's work. Paul states in the Bible in the book of 2nd Thessalonians 3:10, that they had given a rule "The one who is unwilling to work shall not eat." This indicates that all people must be engaged in some work, since all people must eat to live. The work we do can be varied and may not necessarily be formal.

The work we do must foremost be morally right. A thief or drug dealer may also count their activity as work; however, such work is firstly illegal and is morally wrong according to the Bible and must be refrained from. Furthermore, the work we do must better and do good, in a small or great measure, to the world we live in. Work that causes people to sin should be avoided.

The various talents and giftings present in an individual are deposited in them by God as an early indicator and directional guidepost for the type of career and work they should be engaged it. When one's gifts and talents align with the work the person is engaged in, it will be a joyful activity and will have better chances of success. Education helps in identification of both the gifts and the pursuit of training in careers that hone and develop such gifts.

Due to the various circumstances and life choices affecting career choices, not everyone ends up in careers that align with their innate skills and talents. However, it is important to note that all work, whether paid or unpaid, formal or informal as long as it is necessary and is beneficial to our world, has its own dignity and value.

At any workplace, one may encounter employees performing various roles and shouldering various responsibilities. The world we live in typically provides more respect to those at the top, in power and carrying more authority than those further down the organizational structure. However, it is important for us all to treat everyone with respect, irrespective of their authority or position.

While we may receive a salary for our work, the work we do is mostly for others. What we offer are our services. The word service means serving. Most people in deriving a service try to obtain it in the pattern of slavery. This is an age-old practice of obtaining service from others by force. People reluctantly or under compulsion are made to do a task. Since such conditions necessitated brutality, the attitude of both the master and slave reflected hate, fear and other negative attitudes.

This is also particularly important for those in positions of power and authority. The nature to lord it over others because of their position is a temptation that affects all people. In such cases, we look to the Lord Jesus, who though being Lord, is humble to wash the feet of His disciples. The understanding that an elevated position is a responsibility to serve those below them to achieve the organizational goal is yet to be properly understood and realized. The great wisdom exhibited by the lord Jesus in modeling this kind of service shows that by serving the organization by respecting and valuing the staff who work alongside you and below you, only helps in your elevation as a true leader worthy of following. Also, it helps to build an awareness that at the very top, we are serving the Lord who is the ultimate 'Boss' of every structure on this earth.

If in one word we need to know how to behave at work, it should be summed up in the word ' Respect'.

STORY: Joe's vocation took him to different work environments. The first one was a confusing one in his opinion. He was asked to do things by his superiors and blamed for doing them as well. He quickly understood the nature of the work environments as being controlled by forces greater than the individuals who work there. On how keeping up an appearance of working seems more important than the work itself.

Nevertheless, he learned the value of work. Of being competent to fulfill requirements for others. How one's skill can be used as a blessing for others. While most of our vocations are to benefit someone else, joe understood the value of working to bless others.

When Joe saw Christ's attitude of humbly and willingly serving others, he was touched. He also adopted Christ's pattern of the greatest being the lowest. Willing service without a selfish sense of taking advantage of another was a tenet Joe learned from Christ. Joe lives by the sense that everyone can win at work, and no one needs to lose to complete any task successfully.

Chapter Summary/Key Takeaways

When behaving at Work:

- Know that Work is a privilege and a responsibility.
- All people must be engaged in some work, whether paid or unpaid. All work has its own dignity.
- It is important for us all to treat everyone with respect, irrespective of their authority or position.
- At the very top, we are serving the Lord who is the ultimate 'Boss' of every structure on this earth.

In the next chapter, you will learn…

How to behave at School.

8 AT SCHOOL

School is one of those places that are underemphasized for the personal development of an individual. For children today, school quickly turns into a second home. Whatever the child does not learn from home, the child learns from school. School introduces children to teachers and a formal method of teaching that the child may not have encountered at home.

As stated in our earlier chapter on children, once Children understand the concept of learning at home and have developed some basic learning skills, they will be fully ready to embrace learning at school. School brings children of various interests, intellectual capacities, physical statures, value systems all together in one setting. Children will most likely bring in to school whatever they have learned in their interaction at home.

Just like school becomes a second home, teachers become second parents to the children they teach. Teachers have this huge role to play in society as they take on the role of 2nd parent to the children in their classes. After their own parents, children learn about the adult world through their teachers. Teachers hold the key to make learning fun so that Children want to learn about the world they live in.

Too often teaching becomes all about the syllabus course material and children are left with a distaste for learning instead of curiosity and wonder about the world they live in. Without attention and interest, children generally wither. The same can also be seen in the classroom. Unless the child finds their fire of curiosity stoked and an interest in learning generated, we will only see a cold, uninterested child who then turns their attention to other matters. A rekindling of this fire of curiosity is what every good teacher should aim to achieve. This fire can lead a person to leave meaningless activities behind and focus on what stimulates their imagination.

Interactions between students form the base of what children learn about dealing with society in general. The various experiences, both positive and negative, help children understand the nature of behavior in groups. Peer pressure, acceptance and rejection from friends, being preferred by some, ignored by others etc. are all learnt and experienced in School.

The nature of the modern workplace can also be learnt from school when completing portions, exams , deadlines, projects all come into play. The basic tenet of working hard toward success can also be learnt by the individual when the marks or certifications obtained are usually proportional to the effort expended by the student.

Learning to relate to teachers is learning to relate to authority. Behaving with them must always be with respect. Ultimate Authority in the Bible is with God. God delegates authority to others to represent God's nature so that the world can operate in order. Teachers have been delegated authority by God to teach the young so that they may grow in wisdom and knowledge to enable them to live godly lives. Respecting teachers and their authority is ultimately respecting God himself. So, teachers like parents must be treated with respect.

Classmates and peers are vast and varied, and dealing with them requires wisdom and tact. Friendliness is a quality one needs to hone to a good extent to interact with others at school. At school all people can be termed as searching for significance and acceptance. While in the early years, children interact freely with their peers without much judgement, as they grow older, tend to be choosy about who to make friends with. Children both like to find safety in a group of peers and also prioritize who they call friends, best friends etc.

As teens they want to act grownup and take charge of their lives. Friendships change and are typically maintained with others having similar values, common interests and patterns of thought. At school with others, one must learn to behave with friendliness, wisdom and tact.

STORY: Joe felt his school life was missing something. All his time in school he felt lost. Like he was trying to catch up. He could not tell what the problem was. It may have been that he was a year younger than his classmates since he was admitted early. Anyway, he soon found a sweet spot in being able to do enough to get by. His parents were not particularly pleased about his grades; however, they were not particularly disappointed as well. He could come in the top 10 in his class.

He was gifted musically and artistically. His teachers recognized those gifts and made him participate in cultural and school programs.

He enjoyed them more than studies and while he was doing reasonably well in school, he was more pleased to pursue artistic interests like music, drama, quiz etc. He got good recognition in the school in those spheres.

He participated in a sports quiz in his school. He coincidentally learnt from the very same General Knowledge book that his teacher also selected questions from. He had learnt it so well that he could predict the next question that the teacher was about to ask, he could tell its answer to his friends in advance before the teacher asked it. Their team blew the opposite team out of the competition. His teacher commented later to his parents that if Joe could study the way he studied for the quiz, nothing would be impossible for him in studies.

His college life also continued in the same vein. He excelled in the arts. He imagined his career also was headed in some direction in that sphere. College is where he met Christ. His life did a 180 after that and his pursuits, dreams and even his intellect was turned for the better atter his interaction with Christ.

Chapter Summary/Key Takeaways

When behaving at School:

- Behaving with teachers must always involve respect.
- Teachers are people who have authority delegated to them and learning to respect them is learning to respect authority, noting that the ultimate authority is God.
- At school, one must learn to behave with friendliness, wisdom and tact with others.

In the next chapter, you will learn…

How to behave with Society.

9 WITH SOCIETY

Society is a great leveler. Step out into the street and you will see all sorts of people. Rich, poor, wise, foolish, proud, humble, one can see them all. It puts everyone in its place. Society is made up of people. It may be at work, school, church or in any such setting where an individual may find themselves.

It is necessary for all of us to interact with society since it reveals to us the variety of God's creation even among mankind. Starting from the way we look, think, talk, behave, we can see the vast multitude of human nature and behaviors. While our differences may be many, we also understand that at the core, we are also very alike. For instance, we can all agree that we all want to feel accepted and loved. There is no person who can deny that fact. However much we state that we don't need anyone's love or acceptance, deep down we all crave it.

While the modern world tries to teach us that we do not need anyone to survive and we stive for independence, we simultaneously feel the pangs and need for friendship and acceptance from others. We are wired for love and community. Even if we feel we don't need anyone to live our lives, we can't deny that we are all searching for friends and love.

While in our chapter with God, we have stated that our first call is to love God, the second is to love our neighbor as ourselves. This society is at large our neighbors, and we are called to love them. As ourselves ! We like to draw boundaries to define our society. However, we can all admit that we daily interact with much more people than those we call our friends or preferred people. How should our interaction then be with others in society ?

Too often we see a world where we identify certain hierarchies based on power, money, status etc. and we behave differently with different classes of people. We typically see in this world the rich being treated kindly and the poor with unkindness. The influential are treated with respect and the uninfluential are largely ignored. The powerful are treated with deference and the powerless with scorn and abuse.

If we get the first part/chapter right, we can see that as we learn to love an invisible God, a God who identifies with the lowly and the least in society, we can also learn to love others who are invisible because of

their lack of power, status or wealth. We see that when we value things more than we value people, we treat people in accordance with the measure of their possessions of the things we love. In short, our love for things grows and we only use people as a means to things.
The Bible teaches that we as human beings are created in the image of God. God has created us for eternal life. Those who believe in Jesus Christ will live for eternity in heaven, in the presence of God. Those who reject God will also live in a place separated from God, called hell. So, while things perish, people will all live eternally either with or away from God.

This teaches us the inestimable value of a human soul compared to the temporary perishable things of the world. We must get over our little loves and focus on the bigger love, the love of God and love of people. Now loving people does not mean loving their bodies or lusting after them! Instead, the love of the Bible is a sacrificial love that puts the 'love' of this world to shame.

If we look deep within ourselves, we see that once our basic human needs of food , clothing shelter etc. is met then we turn to matters like significance, fulfillment , purpose. It shows us that our loving others must first be to make sure that such basic needs are met for those who are less privileged. This is an ongoing service all mankind must be engaged in. However, we also see around us people who have their basic needs satisfied but are of varying social standing because of their wealth, influence, power etc. To love all people, we must give them what we ourselves seek, acceptance, dignity, fair treatment, a voice to state our opinion, an ear to hear their words. Too often we give this only to those in power and we end up bitter since we try to use such people for our gain and they in turn use us for their pleasure. Such treatment only leads to abuse of some sort.

We should start valuing people for who they are, people created in God's image, with a capacity for love and friendship. When we see people as eternal beings who have great resources of love, wisdom and worth within them, we will begin to look away from their temporary identities that all people wear like job titles, nationalities etc. Loving people does not necessarily mean that we will be close friends with all people everywhere, but instead that we will treat all people with equal dignity and respect. We will lend an ear to all people and not judge anyone unless we have heard them out and seen their heart.

Society needs to be treated with respect and acceptance but also with wisdom and tact. While the behavior stated above is the preferred norm, most adults have too far lived with the world's system of seeing people as a means to get the things they desire. So, our interaction with people must be fenced with wisdom and tact to properly discern the heart of those we interact with. Nevertheless, we can reach out with acceptance and friendliness to people in society and treating others the way we want to be treated ourselves, it never goes wrong !

STORY: Joe related to people differently prior and post to becoming a believer in Christ. Before he knew Christ, the only person Joe ever cared about deeply was himself. Everything else was secondary. But after knowing Christ, Joe found that in his heart a new love dethroned the self-love and that was the love for Christ. Nothing could be the same again. Joe could always relate to people, being on the sensitive side. But a real concern beyond face value was missing. However, after Christ came into Joe's life, Joe saw people differently. Joe was concerned about people's eternal destiny.

This concern was something God put in Joe's heart. The ability to see the eternal worth of every person in the sight of God. This led Joe to respect all people irrespective of their social standing, financial status, measure of power etc. Now everyone was important, and everyone mattered. This was a liberating experience and something that maintained balance in life.

Chapter Summary/Key Takeaways

When behaving with society:
- Know that people are eternal beings created in God's image.
- Treat others the way we want to be treated ourselves.
- Deal with people with wisdom and tact knowing we live in a broken world.
- Treating others with dignity, friendliness and acceptance never goes wrong.

In the next chapter, you will learn…

How to behave with yourself.

10 WITH YOURSELF

The thought of this chapter may surprise many. Does it matter how I behave with myself? How do I behave with myself? Well to answer that question, to behave with someone, you need to know that someone first. We must first understand who they are. So, to behave with myself, I must first know who I am.

A Christian can understand from the Bible that a human being is a unique creation of God, unlike every other form of life. While living creatures were created by God and have life and God given intelligence and abilities, man alone is distinct. It is written in the Bible that man was made in the image of God.

Man has uniquely a spirit, soul and body. The spirit of man, which is a part of him that is invisible to the physical eye is a part that has the ability to commune with God in the Spirit. A part of man, where God can reside in spirit. Difficult to fathom and comprehend, yet common to all mankind. Each human being is a spiritual being. Every human being has a soul. Again, an invisible part of them, but very active in all mankind. It's the part that comprises of our will, our emotions and intellect. Thirdly, our body is the tangible part of us that interacts with our physical world that houses the soul and spirit.

In order to fully live and take advantage of this world, one must realize this about themselves. The first man, the Bible says had a close communion with God, talked and had fellowship with God in the garden and was spiritually alive. God had given him a command that the day he eats of the fruit of a particular tree of the knowledge of good and evil, he would die. Adam and his wife Eve ate of the fruit disobeying God, but it is noted that they did not physically die that day. But something changed. They who were alive in their spirit, felt a loss of something, a void that made them feel exposed. I consider that they died spiritually that day, because of sin by breaking God's command. The next thing that was affected was their mind. They felt shame and guilt. They could not face God anymore. Since their spiritual connection with God was broken, their mind was the next casualty.

In God's presence, it is noted in Genesis that they partake of blame, fear and other emotions that appeared for the first time in their minds. Now that the spirit was dead, the mind was left untethered to fend for itself. It had no strength to cling on to the spirit, instead it clutched on to protecting itself with reasoning and mental efforts. The body also participated to help the mind ease its pain by taking action like hiding from God, covering itself with leaves etc.

When we talk about the spirit of man, most people will be quick to discount it as mere products of myths or of religious teaching. However, one cannot shake off the feeling that there is a voice of conscience working as a lamp to guide them informing them of the path they need to follow, even though they seem powerless to obey it, instead they find themselves drifting easily into sin. The mind with its emotions, intellect and will are what is stronger in the person, in the absence of the spirit's control. Emotions like fear, guilt, shame, doubt run rampant in the mind and sins's desires like lust, greed, jealousy, envy also run amok ruling both the mind and body.

In short, the person feels enslaved to sin and its passions. It is to break this stranglehold of sin and death of the spirit that Jesus, who was God in the flesh, came to the earth. Because He had not broken a single law of God and remained sinless but was also the righteousness of God completely fulfilling and obeying God's word, his death on the cross has paid the full price of the sin of the world committed due to its disobedience. Any person who accepts this sacrifice on the cross by faith is counted as righteous and forgiven of their sin. Such a person is born again, i.e. their spirit comes to life just as the first man and woman in the garden before their sin. This life in the spirit, is a restoring of the original order in man. Now they are able to commune with God in the spirit and their mind can now be brought under control of the spirit. The body duly obeys the mind. The right order is restored.

When the love for God is paramount and prioritized, the healing of the person begins. Where God is, there is love. Where God is, there is heaven. When God comes to reside inside a believer, there the creation order is restored, and peace is present. Guilt and shame have no reason to be there anymore since the believer relies on the sinless one, Jesus for his righteousness. Fear has no reason to stay since God who knows all things has declared the believer as accepted and forgiven.

It is in this setting that the believer can come into the true acceptance of his place in the family of God. To truly belong to God's family and to have the spirit of God attesting to your spirit that you are a child of God is one of the greatest joys that any person can enjoy in this life. The overflowing love of God fills to capacity, overflowing one's reservoir of love present in the human heart. We can behave toward ourselves with acceptance and due understanding.

While we remain on earth, we must not forget that we still live among broken people, in a lost world and with an enemy of our souls at large. While we treat ourselves with respect, knowing that our spirits are renewed, our minds transformed day by day and our bodies are the temple of the Holy spirit, we still must not forget that our flesh and mind still given the chance can insist on its old patterns and fall prey to sin. Hence it is important to only trust in God on a moment-by-moment basis to lead us to victory until we see him face to face.

STORY: Joe loved himself all his life. Joe was his own biggest fan. Joe always held Joe in great regard. Joe never thought he could love anyone more than himself. He was wrong. Upon giving his heart to Jesus, Joe found that his heart was rewired. Even his love for himself was taking second place to Christ. Though it was difficult to explain, Joe stopped being the center of his own world.

His world had shifted. This was a relief to Joe deep down. He never really believed that he was the center of the world he lived in. A self-satisfying life he found was not a fulfilling one. When Christ came into the center, life suddenly had purpose and meaning. How in giving up one could gain or by humbling oneself, one was exalted, now became a little bit clearer.

Joe loved himself alright, but not like before. He loved Christ more. No turning back.

Chapter Summary/Key Takeaways

When behaving with yourself:
- Know the story of your redemption.
- Accept Christ for your restoration.
- Accept Christ's healing for your renewal.
- Trust only in Christ for your salvation and put no hope in the flesh.

EPILOGUE/CONCLUSION

This book is intended to give you a glimpse of who you are in Christ and how to behave both with God and with the world.

I trust that the reading has been easy and meaningful. No book of this sort is useful if it only affects the mind and does not cause you to any change in your heart and practice.

Take the time to sit with Jesus and ask Him to come into your heart. He is knocking on the door of your heart and waiting for you to open. Only His entry and residence within your heart can turn your heart into heaven. This will, as a result, teach you to behave both with God and Man.

Learning to behave with God is the first step to learning to behave with the world at large. Once we learn to interact and behave with God, we can behave rightly with others. The others indicated in this book are Parents, Spouse, Children, friends, the Church, Work, School, Society and yourself. This list is by no means exhaustive, but only a start to get you thinking about how to interact with your world.

Know that what is expected of you is not an artificial act of conformance but a natural result of God's life within you, which will lead to glory and praise to God as you behave well in every sphere of life !

So have a wonderful life !! Blessings !!!

BIBLIOGRAPHY

Bible References

Chapter 1

    1. Mathew 22: 36-40

    2. 1 John 4: 16

    3. 1 John 4: 19

Chapter 3

    1. Luke 5: 33-35

    2. Ephesians 5: 25-27

    3. Ephesians 5: 22

    4. 1 Peter 3: 1

Chapter 4

    1. Proverbs 22: 6

ABOUT THE AUTHOR

Bobby Kurien is a child of God, who found Christ during his college days in MIT, Manipal, Karnataka, India.

Born and raised in Kuwait, he moved to India for his higher Education in 1990. After earning a degree in Engineering from MIT Manipal, Bobby returned to Kuwait to pursue a career in Engineering.

In addition to writing, Bobby is actively involved in his local church and community, especially the Sunday School Ministry in which he has been involved as a teacher for over 24 years.

Bobby currently resides in Kuwait with his family where they continue to serve Christ through the Sunday School and other various ministries. This is his first literary effort and hopes that this will be the first of many such endeavors.

Printed in Great Britain
by Amazon